"What Can I GET Her?"

Successful Shopping for Your Special Person

A Man's Shopping Guide

Richard Avdoian

What Can I Get Her?
Successful Shopping for Your Special Person
A Man's Shopping Guide

Richard Avdoian
Falls Street Press

Published by Falls Street Press, St. Louis, MO
Copyright © 2022 by Richard Avdoian
All rights reserved.

Cover Design and Interior Layout: Davis Creative

First Edition 2022

Library of Congress Control Number: 2022900257
ISBN: 9798985515800
BISAC Subject headings:
  1. REF015000   Reference / Personal & Practical Guides
  2. REF035000   Reference / Planners

Published in the United States of America

DEDICATION

To the women in my family
Lucille and Mary

Nancy, Christina, Deborah, Pamela,
Takouhie, Rosie, Lori, Katherine, Karine,
Andrea, Jennifer and Lindsey

Special Thanks

Barbara Glanz for her friendship, support, and
encouragement to create this guide.

Jack Davis, for his patience, expertise,
and assistance.

What people are saying...

"I believe every male in the world should have this book, whether for a girlfriend, wife, mother, grandma, sister or aunt...or any other special female in his life. It will save time, mistakes, disappointments, and perhaps even a relationship! Selfishly, I plan to give one to every guy in my close circle of friends and family. Be sure to get it in time for all those special occasions that might have been goofed up in the past!" ;-)

–Barbara Glanz, Hall of Fame Speaker and the author of "The Simple Truths of Service Inspired by Johnny the Bagger," "CARE Packages for the Workplace," and "CARE Packages for the Home."

"Food, water, shelter, clothing...and Richard Avdoian's book, "What Can I Get Her?" Successful Shopping for Your Special Person/A Man's Shopping Guide. All of these are the necessities of life! Now go get this book!!"

–Mikki Williams, Hall of Fame Speaker, TEDx speaker, Executive Speech Coach, Vistage Master Chair and Award-Winning Speaker

"Being a woman, you are lucky to have someone who surprises you with gifts. You are even luckier if this person follows Richard's guide to shower you with things you will cherish forever — from the best anniversary gifts to the right romantic getaway. While your gifts must come from your heart, the inspiration will come from this book."

–Sylvie di Giusto, CSP, Keynote Speaker

For _____

_____
_____
_____
_____
_____
_____
_____
_____
_____
_____

_____

Forward

When Richard first told me about the idea for this book at a conference we were attending, I was EXCITED and selfishly really wanting him to do this for every female in the world who has been constantly disappointed with the gifts she has received from various males throughout her lifetime. I remember one Christmas especially when my husband gave me a VACUUM—I was so upset, the next year I gave him a SHOVEL! Many men have sent me roses, for example, but I would so much rather have an arrangement or flowers like lilies that do not die in 3 days. I just wish they would ask.

Don't get me wrong—I am both a shopper and a giver. I love to buy things for people, and I love when someone gifts me with something, However, it means so much more if there was thought and effort put into it, and I can tell it was purchased just for ME.

Let's face it—most men are NOT shoppers. They go in and usually buy one of the first things they see with very little thought. And then, nine times out of ten, the woman has to take it back. With this guide it will be easy for a man to buy something that his female companion really wants AND in the right size. It will save time, disappoint-ments, and may even save a shaky relationship when the woman is blown away with his personal choices for her.

The Guide can either be filled out by the woman her-self or it is something that can be done together over time. It can even be done in a rather "sneaky" way to surprise her. Ask her friends, look in her closet, if she has a special store or salesperson, contact them, or simply ask some questions now and then and then WRITE THEM DOWN. I guarantee if you use Richard's book, it will enhance your female relationships and you will come out a HERO! Happy shopping!

–Barbara Glanz,
Hall of Fame Speaker and the author of
"The Simple Truths of Service Inspired by Johnny the Bagger," "CARE Packages for the Workplace," and "CARE Packages for the Home.

Contents

Dates to Remember

Wedding Anniversary _____

Anniversary Gifts......on page 45

First Date_____

Birthdays _____

Wife/Significant other _____

Children

Name_____	Date _____
Name_____	Date _____
Name_____	Date _____
Name_____	Date _____
Name_____	Date _____
Name_____	Date _____

Parents

Mom _____ Dad_____

In-Laws

Mom _____ Dad_____

Clothing Sizes

Dress _____   Jean _____

Skirt _____   Pant size _____

Blouse size_____

Jacket size _____   Coat size _____

Favorite designers

_____   _____

_____   _____

_____   _____

Favorite stores

_____   _____

_____   _____

_____   _____

Active Wear

Short/Capri size _____

Tank/Tee shirt top size _____

Favorite Brands

_____   _____

_____   _____

_____   _____

Color Preferences

_____   _____

_____   _____

_____   _____

Notes:

Lingerie

Bra size _____

Favorite Brands

_____   _____

_____   _____

Color Preferences

_____   _____

_____   _____

_____   _____

Nightgown size _____

Preference

☐ Nylon   ☐ Silk   ☐ Cotton   ☐ Blend

Panty size _____

Preference

☐ Nylon   ☐ Silk   ☐ Cotton   ☐ Blend

Foot Wear

	Size	Color	Material
High Heels	_____	_____	_____
Boots	_____	_____	_____
Sandals	_____	_____	_____
Flats	_____	_____	_____
Athletic	_____	_____	_____
Slippers	_____	_____	_____
Socks	_____	_____	_____

Preferred Brand/Designers

_____   _____

_____   _____

_____   _____

Notes:

Handbags & Totes

	Color	Material	Style
Cross Body	_____	_____	_____
Shoulder Bag	_____	_____	_____
Clutch	_____	_____	_____
Evening Bag	_____	_____	_____
Tote	_____	_____	_____
Wallet	_____	_____	_____

Preferred Brand/Designers

_____   _____

_____   _____

_____   _____

Notes:

Flowers

Favorite   Color

_____   _____

_____   _____

_____   _____

Trees/Bushes

_____   _____

_____   _____

_____   _____

Notes:

Jewelry

Earrings

☐ Pierced   ☐ Clip-on   ☐ Either

Color Preference:

☐ Gold   ☐ Silver   ☐ Rose Gold   ☐ Two Tone

Type:

☐ Stud   ☐ Cocktail   ☐ Drop

☐ Tear Drop   ☐ Hoop   ☐ Chandelier

☐ Dangles   ☐ Climber

Bracelet

Size: ☐ S (7 inch)

   ☐ M (7.5 inch)

   ☐ L (8 inch)

   ☐ XL (9 inch)

Preference

☐ Gold   ☐ Silver   ☐ Rose Gold   ☐ Two Tone

Birthstone _____

Favorite Stones/Gems

_____

_____

_____

Necklace

Preferred lengths

☐ (16 inch)   ☐ (18 inch)

☐ (20 inch)   ☐ (24 inch)

☐ (26 inch)   ☐ (30 inch)

Color Preference

☐ Gold   ☐ Silver   ☐ Rose Gold   ☐ Two Tone

Ring sizes

☐ Thumb _____   ☐ Index _____

☐ Middle _____   ☐ Ring _____

☐ Pinkie _____

Spa Treatments I like:

Tanning Spa: _____

Number: _____

Hair Salon: _____

Number: _____

Nail Salon: _____

Number: _____

Massage: _____

Number: _____

Facials: _____

Number: _____

Scrub: _____

Number: _____

Fragrances

Brand _____

Fragrance _____

   ☐ Perfume   ☐ Eau de toilette

   ☐ Lotion   ☐ Bath gel

Brand _____

Fragrance _____

   ☐ Perfume   ☐ Eau de toilette

   ☐ Lotion   ☐ Bath gel

Brand _____

Fragrance _____

   ☐ Perfume   ☐ Eau de toilette

   ☐ Lotion   ☐ Bath gel

Books

☐ Hard copy ☐ Paperback
☐ Audio book

Favorite Authors

_____   _____

_____   _____

_____   _____

Favorite Genre

_____   _____

_____   _____

_____   _____

Books Wish List

_____

_____

_____

_____

_____

Music

Favorite Singers

_____   _____

_____   _____

_____   _____

Favorite Groups

_____   _____

_____   _____

_____   _____

Musicals

_____

_____

_____

Music Wish List

_____

_____

_____

Movies/TV Series

☐ Box DVD   ☐ Box BlueRay

Wish List

_____

_____

_____

_____

_____

_____

_____

_____

_____

_____

_____

_____

_____

_____

_____

_____

Electronics I would like…

☐ Tablet   Brand _____

                Type_____

☐ Laptop   Brand _____

                Type_____

☐ Camera   Brand _____

                Type_____

                Model _____

Other camera equipment

_____   _____

_____   _____

_____   _____

Electronics I would like... (continued)

☐ Phone   Brand _____

                  Model _____

Accessories

_____   _____

_____   _____

_____   _____

☐ eReader   Brand _____

                  Type_____

                  Model _____

☐ MP3 Player Brand _____

                  Model _____

Accessories

_____

_____

_____

Collectibles

I collect

_____   _____

_____   _____

_____   _____

Specialty Shops

_____

Phone number: _____

_____

Phone number: _____

_____

Phone number: _____

Notes:

Candles

Favorite Scents

_____   _____

_____   _____

Candle Size & Shapes (? need)

_____   _____

_____   _____

Accessories

_____   _____

_____   _____

Specialty Shops

_____

Phone number: _____

_____

Phone number: _____

_____

Phone number: _____

My Hobbies

_____

_____

_____

_____

Supply Stores

_____

Phone number: _____

_____

Phone number: _____

_____

Phone number: _____

Misc.

_____

_____

_____

_____

_____

_____

Food & Libations

Restaurant Favorites

_____

_____

_____

_____

_____

Coffee Shop Favorites

_____

_____

_____

_____

Libations Favorite Drinks & Establishments

Wine _____   _____

Cocktail _____   _____

After Dinner _____   _____

Entertainment

Favorite film genres

_____   _____

_____   _____

_____   _____

Live Performances I would like see...

_____

_____

_____

Sporting Events I enjoy...

_____

_____

_____

Stand–Up comics I would like to see

_____

_____

_____

Theater

Plays I would like to see

_____

_____

_____

_____

Musicals I would like to see

_____

_____

_____

_____

Dance Performances I would like to see

_____

_____

_____

_____

Miscellaneous

I would love to have…

- _____

_____

_____

- _____

_____

_____

- _____

_____

_____

- _____

_____

_____

- _____

_____

_____

- _____

_____

_____

A Few Ideal Weekend Getaways would be to...

- _____
  _____
  _____
  _____
  _____
  _____

- _____
  _____
  _____
  _____
  _____
  _____

- _____
  _____
  _____
  _____
  _____
  _____

My ideal day with the family would be…

- _____
_____
_____
_____
_____
_____
_____

- _____
_____
_____
_____
_____
_____
_____

- _____
_____
_____
_____
_____
_____

My Ideal day "Alone" would be...

- _____
  _____
  _____
  _____
  _____
  _____

- _____
  _____
  _____
  _____
  _____
  _____

- _____
  _____
  _____
  _____
  _____
  _____

Ideal Romantic Evenings with you would be:

- _____
_____
_____
_____
_____
_____
_____

- _____
_____
_____
_____
_____
_____
_____

- _____
_____
_____
_____
_____
_____

An Ideal day with you would be:

- _____
_____
_____
_____
_____
_____
_____

- _____
_____
_____
_____
_____
_____
_____

- _____
_____
_____
_____
_____
_____
_____

When I want to celebrate, I'd like...

- _____
_____
_____
_____
_____
_____
_____

- _____
_____
_____
_____
_____
_____
_____

- _____
_____
_____
_____
_____
_____

When I'm stressed and not feeling well, I would like…

- _____
  _____
  _____
  _____
  _____
  _____

- _____
  _____
  _____
  _____
  _____
  _____

- _____
  _____
  _____
  _____
  _____
  _____

For a Perfect Day, I would need...

- _____
  _____
  _____
  _____
  _____
  _____

- _____
  _____
  _____
  _____
  _____
  _____

- _____
  _____
  _____
  _____
  _____
  _____

I would like the following for the Home…

- _____
  _____
- _____
  _____
- _____
  _____
- _____
  _____
- _____
  _____
- _____
  _____
- _____
  _____
- _____
  _____
- _____
  _____
- _____
  _____

Birth Stone

January: Garnet

February: Amethyst

March: Aquamarine

April: Diamond

May: Emerald

June Pearls

July: Ruby

August: Peridot

September: Sapphire

October: Opal

November: Citrine

December: Blue Topaz

Zodiac Birth Signs

Aquarius (January 20 – February 18)

Pisces (February 19 – March 20)

Aries (March 21 – April 19)

Taurus (April 20 – May 20)

Gemini (May 21 – June 20)

Cancer (June 21 – July 22)

Leo (July 23 – August 22)

Virgo (August 23 – September 22)

Libra (September 23 – October 22)

Scorpio (October 23 – November 21

Sagittarius (November 22 – December 21)

Capricorn (December 22 – January 19)

Wedding Anniversary Gifts by Year

1st Anniversary: Paper

2nd Anniversary: Cotton

3rd Anniversary: Leather

4th Anniversary: Fruit or Flowers

5th Anniversary: Wood

6th Anniversary: Candy or Iron

7th Anniversary: Wool or Copper

8th Anniversary: Pottery or Bronze

9th Anniversary: Willow or Pottery

10th Anniversary: Tin or Aluminum

11th Anniversary: Steel

12th Anniversary: Silk or Linen

13th Anniversary: Lace

14th Anniversary: Gold Jewelry

15th Anniversary: Crystal

16th Anniversary: Coffee or Tea

17th Anniversary: Wine or Spirits

18th Anniversary: Appliances

19th Anniversary: Jade

20th Anniversary: China

21st Anniversary: Fire (theme)

22nd Anniversary: Water (theme)

23rd Anniversary: Air (theme)

24th Anniversary: Stone (theme)

25th Anniversary: Silver

26th Anniversary: Art

27th Anniversary: Music

28th Anniversary: Linens

29th Anniversary: Tools

30th Anniversary: Pearls

31st Anniversary: Travel

32nd Anniversary: Bronze

33rd Anniversary: Iron

34th Anniversary: Food

35th Anniversary: Coral

36th Anniversary: Antiques

37th Anniversary: Books

38th Anniversary: Luck (theme)

39th Anniversary: Laughter (theme)

40th Anniversary: Ruby

41st Anniversary: Office or Desk Decor

42nd Anniversary: Clocks or Watches

43rd Anniversary: Entertainment (theme)

44rd Anniversary: Electronics (theme)

45th Anniversary: Sapphire

46th Anniversary: Games

47th Anniversary: Garden or Plants

48th Anniversary: Home Improvement (theme)

49th Anniversary: Copper

50th Anniversary: Gold

51st Anniversary: Photos or Cameras

52nd Anniversary: Bath or Spa (theme)

53rd Anniversary: Plastic

54th Anniversary: Glass

55th Anniversary: Emerald

56th Anniversary: Day (theme)

57th Anniversary: Night (theme)

58th Anniversary: Faith and Hope (theme)

59th Anniversary: Charity (theme)

60th Anniversary: Diamond

About the Author

Richard J. Avdoian, CSP™, MS, MSW

Richard is a pioneer in "Men's Work" helping men to develop a deeper understanding of masculinity. Drawing on his years in private practice as a psychotherapist, Richard founded the Men Mentoring Men Network and Voyager Men's Experience to challenge and inspire men to achieve a healthier life, enhance relationships and reach their full potential.

Richard Avdoian is founder and CEO of Midwest Business Institute, Metro St. Louis a leadership coaching, consulting, and training group.

He works with businesses, corporations and associations committed to training and retaining highly motivated, engaged productive employees. He is an employee development expert who specializes in enhancing employee potential and maximizing capabilities to provide exemplary customer service and increase productivity and profitability.

He has worked in the health care field and with clients in over forty different industries proving program and services in teamwork, leadership, and employee development.

Avdoian's credentials rank him among the top speakers in the United States and he is sought out by numerous states, corporations and associations to offer his expertise and insight related to enhancing human potential.

To purchase copies of "What Can I Get Her?"
or other books and products contact Richard at
Richard@RichardAvdoian.com.

Interested in having Richard speak or present training
to your company, corporation or association and
learn more about his programs and services visit
www.RichardAvdoian.com

www.ingramcontent.com/pod-product-compliance
Lightning Source LLC
Chambersburg PA
CBHW060259030426
42335CB00014B/1770